Collectable
Glass

BY JANE DOUGLAS

LONGACRE PRESS
LONDON

First published 1961 by
Longacre Press Ltd.
161–166 Fleet Street, London, E.C.4.
Made in Great Britain at the Pitman Press, Bath

Contents

Introduction

HERE are some ideas on making your own collection of glass. This little book is a companion piece to one on *Collectable China* and it sets out to show that the world of glass can be no less exciting and beautiful than that of china. It tries to give you some facts about the sort of things you can buy in the antique shops, stalls and at sales, and suggests how you could make a collection of, say, decanters, goblets or fancy Victorian coloured glass a truly decorative part of your home.

Some of the items dealt with here cost many pounds and you may have to be content to look at them in the museums: but there are plenty which cost only shillings or just a few pounds. Either way, your collection will surely increase in value. But do not be too much influenced by the value other people put on things; the best way of making a collection and of enjoying it is to trust to your own eye and taste.

JANE DOUGLAS

1. *English Flint Glass*

Shapes

TODAY, people seem to prefer colour in glass, as in other things. But there are many pleasures to be had from clear English flint glass in its various forms, especially that of the eighteenth and early nineteenth centuries.

Sand has long since replaced flint pepples in our glass, but this is the term we still use for all that wonderful glass, full of lead, with its beautiful watery texture, which makes you think of liquefied light made solid. It may not have been so manageable as the glass of other countries, but its great quality was its capacity for holding and dispersing light. If you are going to collect any of it your first task must be to get to know the difference between this material and the lighter, and actually more brilliant, material being made today. The only way to do this is to go to the museums and look at it, attend sales and handle it, talk to the more knowledgeable dealers—there are specialists in this field—and get to know other collectors.

Next you must consider the various ways in which the beauty of this material can be enhanced. You can engrave it with a diamond, point or a little wheel; you can cut it, shallow or deep, on a larger wheel; you can etch a pattern on it with acid as in copper plate printing; and you can enamel it either in white or in colours.

Cut Glass

IN the best period of English glass the makers were so proud of their material that their object was not so much to gild this very lovely lily with extraneous decoration, as other countries did with theirs, but to bring out its own fine qualities. So they cut it into patterns on the wheel, not merely to give interest to its shape, but to provide extra surfaces and angles which would catch the light and give a piece that internal fire which is the joy of collectors.

The heyday of cut glass was in the years 1780 to about 1840, during the time when many of the English glass makers crossed to Ireland to avoid the heavy excise duties on their raw materials. It was then, with cheaper materials making heavier vessels possible, that there developed the very deep cutting which most people now associate with cut glass. Many collectors prefer the shallower and more restrained cutting of the early and mid-eighteenth century, and there was also a revival of this in the second half of the nineteenth century, for which Ruskin is said to have been responsible. However, this is a matter of taste and selection—also of money, for if the heavily cut glass is dear the earlier styles can be dearer still.

The best way to get to know about deep cut glass is to go to Stourbridge or some other glassmaking centre and watch how the job is done. There is not a great deal of difference between today's methods and those of the eighteenth century. You can see them mark out the pattern with red paint—often done by women—then do the first "rough" cut, then smooth and polish. You will notice that in some places the glassmakers are reproducing virtual replicas of the old wares, either by cutting entirely or by pressing out a pattern and then sharpening it up with some cutting here and there. This means that unless you get to know about cuts, and the differences between old and modern glass, you may be buying shop goods at the price of antiques. You will also realise that there is a very definite limit to the number of different types of cut one can make with a wheel, and this will help you a great deal in distinguishing cut glass from pressed glass.

If you look at the old glass—and there is plenty about at the bigger sales—you will find that there are a number of motifs built up from the basic cuts. There are sprigs and fans, stars and relief diamonds. There are "strawberry" diamonds, with a square of little diamonds in the centre;

(*Left*) A cut glass cream jug which could be either English or Irish. (*Centre*) A cut glass jug attributed to one of the Irish glasshouses. (*Right*) A very lightly cut engraved decanter. All three pieces date from the early nineteenth century (*Victoria and Albert Museum*).

there is the familiar "hobnail" pattern with a star in the centre of a square. There are also curved patterns showing circles and semicircles and ovals. But all of these, however ingeniously combined, are built up from the basic cuts.

You hear many people talk of "Irish" glass as though it was something totally different from English glass. It might save a good deal of confusion if we called all this glass "Anglo-Irish," for as already mentioned, the glass made in Ireland at the height of the cut-glass period was a joint effort. There are authenticated specimens of glass made in the Irish factories like Cork, Waterford and Dublin, but much the same types were being made in England from the same materials at the same time.

There is also the Waterford legend. For many years it was believed that the blue tinge in the glass was an infallible indication of manufacture at Waterford. But it has now been shown that whereas a lot of identifiable Waterford *has* got a blue tinge, there is just as much glass from elsewhere which has, too.

Engraved Glass

COLLECTORS of engraved glass consider themselves above what some of them call the "cut and slash" school. This may be because some early engraved glass is very expensive nowadays, possibly also because, on the whole, engraving is far more difficult to do, and calls for an artist as much as a craftsman.

Probably the most famous of the English engraved glasses are the Jacobites. When the Stuarts were driven out, their supporters in this country formed themselves into clubs and societies, which met to dine and drink the health of the banished dynasty. They used table glass decorated with symbols: a rose with six, seven or eight petals, a star, the oakleaf, butterflies, and various flowers. Some bear the word "Fiat" ("So be it") or other mottoes, and verses with the word "Amen" (see page 11).

All these glasses are very costly indeed nowadays, and certainly not for the collector of limited means. But as there is usually a great deal of controversy about the meaning of the symbols it may be interesting to give the current versions. It is now thought that the rose itself represents the crown, or Britain, and a single bud the Old Pretender. Two buds is supposed to indicate both Pretenders, i.e. James Edward and Charles Edward. There is some disagreement about which bud represents which Pretender, and some hold that a single bud on later glasses represents the Young Pretender after the death of his father. Nearly everyone seems nowadays to reject the idea that one of the buds represents Prince Henry, the younger son of the Old Pretender, who became a cardinal. There are also glasses with portraits of the Stuart exiles, some of them crude. Flowers like forget-me-nots, daffodils and carnations are thought to bear meanings—but this is highly specialist stuff, and those interested are referred to the experts.

(*Left*) A rummer with cup-shaped bowl engraved with a design of hops and barley. 5⅞ in. high. Made about 1800–1825 (*Victoria and Albert Museum*). (*Right*) Engraved vase of about 1870–1880 (*Victoria and Albert Museum*). (*Below, left and right*) Back and front views of a mid-eighteenth century "Jacobite" wine glass (see page 9) showing (*left*) a wheel-engraved portrait of Prince Charles Edward Stuart, the Young Pretender and the motto "Audentior Ibo" ("I will go boldly"). On the other side (*right*) are typical Jacobite emblems of a rose with a single bud and a thistle. This glass is also an example of an "air-twist" stemmed glass, as described on page 20 (*Victoria and Albert Museum*).

Still far from cheap, but all the same reasonably obtainable is the "flowered" glass of the mid-eighteenth century. This word is rather misleading, perhaps, for the "flowers" are usually hop vines and barley on ale glasses and grapes and vine leaves on wine glasses; these motifs have been used right down to the present day (see goblet on page 10). Another sort of engraved glass commemorates military and naval victories, as did the pottery of the time, also such engineering triumphs as the building of the Iron Bridge, Sunderland, which figures on so much lustre pottery. Recently I saw come up for auction a rummer engraved with a mail coach and inscribed "Lord Nelson York and London," apparently the name of a mail coach, for on the other side the engraver wished success not only to the town and trade of York, but also

> Success to the Swan (an Inn of great call)
> No better accommodation in England at all.

It made as much as thirty pounds, and one hopes it will one day find itself back in the still existing "White Swan" at York.

These commemorative glasses fetch high prices, more perhaps than they are really worth, simply considered as works of the engraver's skill. Personally, after the "flowered" glasses I prefer those with fox hunting and other sporting scenes—beloved of the age in pottery and prints as well. Somehow English craftsmen are always far more at home with animal subjects, whatever medium they are working in.

The three wine glasses on the opposite page show some of the first patterns produced by the "geometrical" etching machine invented by John Northwood about 1865. The machine worked with trains of copper etching wheels operated by different shaped cams and levers. On the left is the ever popular "key" pattern, while the two others show later variations. Sometimes freehand work was added (*Pictures from "John Northwood," by John Northwood II*).

Etched Glass

AFTER engraving comes etching—or as some people call it, acid engraving. This brings us down to the nineteenth century (we can forget about the early uses of it on the Continent) and all those pleasant festoons of flowers and geometrical designs which the Stourbridge glassmakers devised in the second half of the nineteenth century. These can be very collectable indeed, and at no exorbitant price.

Etching is based on the action of hydrofluoric acid on glass. The piece is first coated with wax, then the design is drawn with a steel-pointed stiletto: the acid eats into the part not covered by wax, and bites in the design. The invention of a machine for automatic etching in 1861 by the famous John Northwood made the process very popular indeed, and although these early designs were at first limited to the still popular "key" and "circle" patterns, they later became very free and ungeometrical.

But the finest work of this kind are those pieces etched with templates—another invention of the Northwoods—whereby transfers were taken from tinfoil plates cut by hand. There are many thousands of these designs, from simple ones of flowers, birds, ferns, butterflies to complete pictures in the Greek Renaissance or Egyptian styles, and some were finished off by hand engraving.

Cameo Carving

WHILE discussing the work of the Northwoods one ought to mention their famous cameo carving in glass. John Northwood himself astonished his contemporaries by such triumphs of the glass carver's skill as his reproduction of the Portland Vase and other pieces. They were made by "casing" an opal glass on to a flint or coloured body, then carving away the opal until the design stood out in relief.

Such pieces as these, which took years to complete and —in the case of the Portland Vase reproduction—cost £1,000 even in 1876, are now quite beyond the reach of the ordinary collector, but later the firm of J. and J. Northwood, of Wordsley, faced with a phenomenal demand for cameo glass, developed a commercial version of it. The hand carving was helped out with engraving on the wheel, and to speed up this work the "casing" was made thinner.

Cameo "blanks" in a whole variety of shapes (see group below) were made by Stevens and Williams, of Brierley Hill, and sent to the Northwood decorating shops at Wordsley for engraving. Some of the designs on this commercial cameo glass follow the classical themes so popular in that day, others have very pleasing patterns of leaves and flowers derived from the naturalistic designs which were also attracting people's attention.

A group of "commercial" cameo glass of the period 1885–1890, by J. and J. Northwood, of Wordsley. From the collection of the Stourbridge Corporation.

Intaglio

EARLY "intaglio" glass is another very collectable Victorian type. This method of decoration, now to be seen everywhere on modern glass, was another development of the Northwoods. "Intaglio" in its general sense, means the opposite of "relief," in that the design does not stand out from the surface but is cut into it, as with a seal.

As applied to glass decoration it was an extension of engraving methods, whereby the engravers, instead of using their little copper grinding wheels, could work with the stone ones, of the sort normally used for cutting, so combining the freedom and flowing lines of the engraver with the deep, lustrous work of the cutter. The process really arose—as so many new developments do—from necessity: the fact that with the decline of public enthusiasm for cameo glass, work had to be found for both engravers and etchers. Many fine pieces are to be found with both etched and intaglio work on them (see page 25). There are also large bowls in the Art Nouveau style which also make use of traditional cutting as well.

Collectors interested in these and other developments should try to get a book called "John Northwood."

Goblet with plume pillar and intaglio decoration. Made about 1900 (*Courtesy Stevens and Williams, Ltd*).

Enamelled Glass

PAINTING glass is not always very successful because unless it is protected in some way, the paint tends to wash off. This you will see with the rolling pins (see "Nailsea") where the painting or gilding is all but unreadable. No doubt many glasses we see now as plain started their life resplendently gilt.

But enamelling, in which a glassy paint is afterwards fired to "fix" the colours is a different matter, and for those with fairly deep purses offers interesting fields of collecting. There is the white opaque glass of Bristol (see facing page) and elsewhere, which tried to look like porcelain not only in its body and colour, but also in styles of decoration, such as flowers and birds and chinoiseries, and was sometimes even done by the same people. These pieces include bottles, beakers, vases, candlesticks, tea canisters, scent bottles, étuis, snuff boxes and a host of other small items.

Another important and even less cheap school of enamelling was that carried out by the Beilby family of Newcastle-on-Tyne, in the last half of the eighteenth century, the subjects being an enamel version of the engraved "flowered" patterns, heraldic designs, or enchanting little vignettes of country scenes and pursuits in the manner of Thomas Bewick, the wood engraver, who in fact at one time worked for the Beilbys. A great deal of European enamelled glass appears in the salerooms, notably German and Bohemian, and some of these styles were followed by English enamellers in the middle nineteenth century. These glasses are well worth looking for now.

(*Right*) A candlestick of beautifully balanced design in the opaque white glass developed at Bristol, and also made in centres like Warrington. This one, made about 1770, has a refined "wrythen" stem, and the flowered decoration is probably by the famous Michael Edkins, who painted procelain and glass at Bristol (*Victoria and Albert Museum*).

Around the Dining-room

S O far we have been talking about the glass itself and the sort of ways in which one can enhance its beauty or interest. Now let us have a look at some of the things which are made of it.

Probably we could not do better than go around a dining-room and see how it was used. There will be plenty of it, and probably most prominent of all, hanging in the centre of the room a great chandelier, with scintillating lustres or "brilliant drops." Few of those seen in the shops today will have survived intact from the eighteenth century without repairs or replacements, but they are still magnificent things, and must have looked glorious in the light of a multitude of candles.

On the tables themselves will be candelabra, with slender branches carrying the candle-sockets, sometimes diamond-cut or scalloped, with heavy bases for stability. There will also be those near relatives which started as simple "vase candlesticks," later to become girandoles with fringes of hanging lustres and finally to evolve into the coloured glass lustre vase of the Victorian mantelshelf.

Then, on the side tables there are the sweetmeat and desert glasses, a brave display meant to impress the guest, and beautifully made little pieces they are. Some are in the same style as the drinking glasses, with restrained cutting to catch the light. They will probably be built up in pyramids on salvers, with a large one—the "captain"—in the middle.

There are many shapes of these little glasses. Sweetmeat glasses proper were often saucer shaped on a stand, rather like our champagne glasses, though much thicker (see page 28). Others came in the shape of boats. Jelly glasses were usually trumpet-shaped, ribbed or gadrooned, sometimes with one or two handles. These can be found in sets, like the custard glasses, which were usually like small cups with handles.

Glass salt cellars (or salts, to use the professional term) came in several different shapes and there are pretty condiment bottles, often with silver mounts which enable you to date them by the hallmark. There were "gimmel" flasks with two intertwined stems for oil and vinegar, and urn-shaped honey pots. Finger bowls were either straight-sided or cup-shaped, some lightly cut: if you come across one with a notch in the rim, this is probably a wine-glass cooler, made so that you could hang your wine glass foot upward in it (see back cover).

Then there will be those wonderful great bowls of cut glass, some tall and slender, some massive and broad. There will be jugs, punch bowls, fruit bowls, salad bowls, stately high-standing bowls with covers. There are some fine ones in the specialist shops at prices which though not low, cannot be considered dear at today's money values, and must always represent a good investment.

DRINKING GLASSES

If we are looking for variety in our collecting subject, we will certainly find it in the department of drinking glasses. You could make not one collection of them, but dozens of different collections, all with excellent sense and logic to them, all equally attractive. Even the eighteenth century would keep you busy—and permanently hard-up— for several lifetimes, while the nineteenth would give you more horizons to reach. All we can do in the compass of this little book is to indicate the various types there are, and suggest how you might find out more about them.

Perhaps the earliest practical types for the collector are those with plain or baluster stems, for these were the styles in existence when English "glass of lead" came into existence in the late seventeenth century.

Never imagine that one baluster stem glass is like any

other baluster stem glass, for they come in shapes as varied as those of the men who made them. The late Mr. E. Barrington Haynes sorted them out into families, genre and species, dealing with hundreds of different kinds with most wonderful patience and logic. They can have upright or inverted balusters, with one or more knops, of different kinds; the bowl could have self-descriptive shapes like cup, bucket, trumpet, flute, ogee, funnel and others; the feet could be variously domed, terraced, folded or oversewn.

These relatively simple glasses were generally made in two pieces, the stems being drawn out to form the bowl. They often have an entrapped bubble or "tear" of glass under the bowl, and this was the origin of the famous "air-twist" so beloved of collectors (see page 11): the "tear" was elaborated into delicate patterns of light. The so-called "mercury" twists, by the way, do not actually hold mercury but are an effect of particularly brilliant glass.

Later this "air-twist" gave place to the even more sought-after "opaque twist" and "colour twist." Here, intricately lacy patterns were made by drawing out canes of white or coloured opaque glass and enfolding them in clear glass: apparently there are more than a hundred different ways in which this can be done. The colours sometimes combined opaque white with yellow, blue, green and ruby.

All these glasses were highly popular until the year 1777, when the Government suddenly put a heavy tax on the enamel glass from which the twists were made. From then on they began to fade out of the picture and were replaced by glasses which were either plain or had light cutting or engraving.

So much for the earlier styles of decorating. Now for the various types of glasses, according to their purpose. Georgian wine glasses come in many styles—our pictures show just a few of these. But the ale-glasses tended to be "flutes," either tall or short, and if both sorts seem small by the standards of today's beer drinkers it should be remembered that eighteenth-century ale was a far more

(*Top left*) Dram glass with a "deceptive" bucket bowl (see page 22) and an annulated or ringed knop in the stem.

(*Top right*) Two-piece wine, with conical bowl. The bowl and stem were drawn out in one piece.

(*Bottom left*) Wine glass with thistle bowl and inverted baluster stem.

(*Bottom right*) Wine glass with fluted trumpet bowl, and six-ribbed pedestal stem. Note that the older the glass the more generous, usually, the foot: this is especially seen in the dram on the front cover with the oversewn foot. The glasses shown above, and on page 23, were bought within the last year or so for prices from 5s. to 25s.

virulent affair than most of those brews we know today. You could, I suppose, classify it as what we would call "stingo."

Delightfully of their period are the cordial glasses, with their tiny bowls on long stems, also the "surfeit" glasses, to carry spirits and cordials designed to revive the over-gorged diner in those days of generous appetites. These have tiny flute-like stems, so that the precious spirit would not easily evaporate.

Special punch and champagne glasses have attractive shapes, and even cider has its own glass. Rummers were bigger glasses, usually with a round, bucket-shaped bowl; their function was to carry "grog" or hot rum and water. If you come across an odd-looking glass which, having no foot, has to stand on its head, do not at first assume that the foot is lost; it may be a coaching glass, brought to waiting travellers and therefore having no more need of a foot than a stirrup cup.

"Deceptive" glasses are always of interest. These are so designed, with careful cutting and shaping, so that what looks like a generous tot is mostly glass reflecting a quite small amount of liquor. They were used by "toastmasters" —not, however, our present gentlemen with loud voices and red coats who announce speakers at banquets, but the host himself, or what we should call the chairman. Since most of these hosts would have been "in the pink," by reason of their daytime activities, one wonders if this is the origin of the modern toastmaster's raiment. Anyway they must have found these glasses very useful when striving manfully to respond to all the toasts which might be offered in the course of the evening. A later use of the same glasses was for landlords called upon by their customers to "have one with me," and at the same time anxious to see that a little brandy went a long way (see page 21).

There is also a very slender-stemmed glass, of which, surprisingly, quite a few have survived, specially intended for snapping between the fingers after toasting a lady.

(*Top left*) Wine glass with conical bowl, hollow stem and slightly domed foot.

(*Top right*) Dwarf ale glass, with wrythen conical or trumpet bowl and short knopped stem.

(*Bottom left*) Regency "pub" or tavern rummer with bucket bowl. A rummer is a more squat affair than a goblet (see page 41) having a shorter stem in relation to height. The word "rummer" seems to derive either from the Dutch "roemer," meaning "Roman," or the lower Rhenish "to boast." But that has not prevented us from using them for hot rum toddy, and so letting them live up to the name.

(*Bottom right*) Victorian "pub" or tavern wine with facetted baluster stem; a thick heavy old glass with no refinement at all, but very pleasant to use compared with some modern ones.

A whole family of glasses have picked up the name "Hogarth" glasses, because of their frequent appearance in engravings by the great artist. They represent the ordinary drinking glasses of the day in tavern or club, and they are usually short, with little or no stem. Apart from the dwarf ales, they include drams, used for very strong liquors, and small gin glasses which are shaped like miniature wines. There is another race with a very thick foot, known as "firing" glasses. Anyone who understands the expression "Kentish Fire" will realise that they were useful for banging on the table in response to a toast—or by way of expressing a wish that they should be filled again as quickly as possible.

Very few genuine eighteenth-century glasses—except the quite plain "taverns"—are now likely to be found anywhere but in the better shops. Most of these, if they are of any quality, then quickly pass into the hands of the specialist dealers and the collectors. At the big auctions at Sothebys, for example, when sold in lots, they can make anything from one to fifteen pounds apiece, with much more for rarities.

In fact this can be a good way of starting off your collection, for the Sotheby cataloguers know their business and are not often deceived. One useful little lot I saw recently included a patch glass with a triple knopped baluster stem and a folded foot, a late firing glass engraved with a frieze of poultry, a short cordial glass and eight other various pieces. It made eight pounds—not a great deal of money.

DECANTERS

Whenever I see a row of decanters in an antique shop I wonder how long it will be before there is a rush to buy them up. I know that many of these are quite ordinary, very cheap affairs, turned out by the hundred thousand in the last fifty years; all the same there are many fine

(*Left*) Late Victorian decanter with etched and also intaglio (see pages 13 and 15) decoration. Made about 1889 (*Courtesy Stourbridge Corporation*). (*Centre*) "Bristol blue" spirit decanter, inscribed "RUM" in gilt. These "labelled" spirit bottles often came in sets of three, for rum, gin and brandy (*Courtesy "bits and pieces"*). (*Right*) Cut-glass "Prussian" shape decanter. Late eighteenth century (*Victoria and Albert Museum*).

ones among them, and not at all dear in comparison with other glass.

It would be an interesting thing indeed to make a collection of decanters which showed their development in colour and in shape through the years, the different sorts of processes they were made in, also the different *kinds* of decanters used for different purposes. For me the obvious way to arrange these would be on open shelves against the light—but before one makes up one's mind about that it might be as well to look and see what sort of decanters one can find.

COLLECTABLE GLASS

If we go back to the eighteenth century—which is as far as we are likely to get anyway—there are the very early shapes—globular with a long neck, or mallet-shaped. There are cylindrical ones with grooves and some have a cruciform shape. The engraving already mentioned in connection with drinking glasses was, of course, done on decanters, too. There were the usual engraved flowers, birds and insects, and often the name of the contents—white wine, rum, hock, port, punch and the rest—within a festoon of stars or some other motif. There were also smaller versions, the so-called taper decanter, and these slim ones were often in blue or green glass with gilt labels and titles. These are not cheap nowadays, and neither are those rare ones enamelled in white. Later, apparently, than tapers came those shaped like a barrel, with vertical flutings for staves and rings for hoops. Another popular shape was called the Prussian; it had a broader shoulder, an inward slope and rings round the neck. The so-called "Royal" shape has sides sloping outwards.

These fairly conventional shapes by no means exhaust possibilities. There are quite square ones, with high shoulders, for packing in cases, some of them small and used for cordials or toilet waters. There are the "Rodneys" —with very wide bases, for use in ships.

As for decoration, some of the finest of the Anglo-Irish cutting went into decanters, while the cased and flashed ruby techniques were also used here, as well as "Mary Gregory" and Nailsea. Some of the early etched or acid engraved ones show very fine work.

Stoppers are a study in themselves, and often help to date a piece. Early ones were spire-shaped, often cut with hollow diamonds, and later came the hollow blown ones, the discs and mushroom shapes.

Some very fine decanters were made quite late in the nineteenth century by the Whitefriars Glasshouses and these are well worth seeking out now.

Personally I would go at decanter collecting in two ways.

(*Above*) Custard glass of a shape used right down to the present day (see page 18).

(*Right*) Jelly glass, cut with ribbed decoration. Made in the first half of the eighteenth century. Jelly and other dessert glasses are mentioned on page 18 (*Victoria and Albert Museum*).

(*Left*) Eighteenth century sweetmeat glass, probably used for syllabub, a popular Georgian dessert made from sherry and cream whipped up into a froth and placed on top of sweetened sherry and claret. And very nice, too! This glass has a "Silesian" stem and domed foot. Note the difference between it and a jelly glass: the wide bowl made it possible for the "froth" to sit on top of the sherry (*Victoria and Albert Museum*).

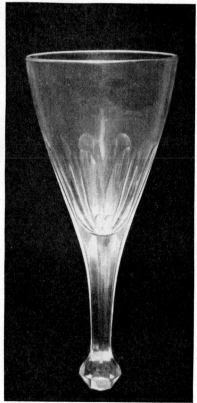

(*Right*) Coaching or stirrup glass, late eighteenth or early nineteenth century. These glasses were used instead of conventional ones when handing hot toddy, or some other comforter, round to passengers in stage coaches or members of the hunt at a meet. The waiter filled you up from a jug. There was no need for a foot as you had nowhere to put the glass down anyway (*Victoria and Albert Museum*).

I would carefully sort out whatever I could find from the Victorian and later pieces—I feel sure more interest will be shown in these as time goes on—then treat myself every now and then to a rarity like a "Bristol" blue taper, a flashed ruby or a fine piece of cutting. Such a collection, with the eccentric shapes as a foil to the more orthodox ones, with the occasional colour being set off by the plain ones, with all of them shined and polished and lit from behind, would be a magnificent thing to have in any room.

WHITEFRIARS

In the last section we briefly mentioned some decanters made by the firm of Powell at the Whitefriars factory in London. With their wavy, undulating lines, or poppy heads they are worth collecting as decanters, and also as examples of a whole class of later English flint glass which could be a most rewarding field for the collector.

The movement seems to have started as a reaction from the heavily cut, sometimes almost prickly, styles shown at the Great Exhibition in 1851. It was probably helped along by a pronouncement by Ruskin that glass was an essentially fluid thing, and oughtn't to be treated like stone and carved deeply. According to him, the glassmakers should concentrate on vessels which relied on the beauty of blown shapes.

Whether Ruskin was responsible or not, there grew up a whole family of late Victorian glass in these styles which does not yet seem to have a name. As much of it was made by Powells, the term Whitefriars may do for a beginning. The interesting thing is that its shapes looked back beyond those of the heavy "glass of lead" of the eighteenth century and seems to carry on the older English tradition which started with Rome and Venice. It also, surprisingly, has something of the feeling—though without its home-made look—of the English country market glass shown on page 33. Designers like Philip Webb, a disciple of William Morris, and Sir Thomas Jackson, an architect, were early in the field, but the style has been carried down to recent times in the work of men like Barnaby Powell, James Hogan and others.

Nothing could be farther removed from conventional cut glass than this work, and one of these days we shall realise how collectable it is—probably when it has all been snapped up by the museums.

ODDMENTS

But while we are still talking about glass types and shapes, do not let us forget all those relatively unconsidered items like inkpots, oil-pots with a long spout for filling lamps, tea and coffee pots, little phials, jars, some of them with ears, in which case they become piggins, and also a whole class of oil lamps. Mr. Bernard Hughes has drawn attention to the fact that many a small piece of glass, thought of as a patch bowl or flower vase or a wafer holder, is actually one of the many little glass lamps used in Georgian days and later. There were some like salt cellars, which originally had a holder for the wick to float in, others had fixed wicks. There were also peg lamps, with nozzles like candles, into which a spherical font carrying the oil was inserted.

Don't overlook some of the more modest examples of early etching, such as cruet bottles, pickle jars and other items.

2. Nailsea and Country Fairings

AT Nailsea in Somerset, as you pass in the train from Bristol to Weston-super-Mare, you can still see a few creeper-covered stumps of buildings on the site of the famous glassworks, which once employed several hundred men.

Nowadays "Nailsea" is a legend, and the word has come to be applied to several different kinds of fancy or coloured glass which were made at other places besides Nailsea, and often long after the factory closed.

First there are all those bottles, jugs, rolling pins, decanters, cups and mugs which are made of dark bottle glass with coloured flecks. Sometimes these flecks are white, sometimes they are in other colours like red, yellow, and pale blue. Either way the effect is charming, and in some mysterious way they go admirably with modern furnishings. They have been eagerly sought after for many years now, and in fact wares very much like them have been made in the quite recent past to satisfy the demand.

Originally they are thought to have been a sort of by-product of a bottle-glass factory at Nailsea in Somerset, at the time when there was a heavy duty on clear glass but none on the darker bottle glass. The opaque glass flecks were said to be the oddments left over from the working of the famous opaque glass made at that time in Bristol. However, very similar things to these were also made in other glassmaking centres like Sunderland, Newcastle, Stourbridge and Wrockwardine, in Shropshire. In fact, yellow flecks are supposed to be a sign of origin at Wrockwardine, though I do not know on what authority, for the name is also given by auctioneers to pieces with white or red flecks. I have also recently seen a bottle with a seal on its holder and with the initials of somebody living in Stirling, so these bottles may even have been made in Scotland, probably Alloa, where a Nailsea man is said to have emigrated.

Then there is a variation of the bottle-glass type which has loops of opaque glass in a style which one can trace back to the ancient Egyptians. This also appeared in some flasks of clear glass. I find these very interesting, since here is the first example of the famous *latticinio* technique (see page 41). With this the glassblower takes a "gather" of molten glass—it looks like a ball of orange toffee—and thrusts it into a mould which has been lined with canes of coloured opaque glass. These fuse into the glass as he blows it with his blow-iron, and he combs the parallel lines down to produce the festooned effect. This technique seems to have arrived in Nailsea when the proprietors imported some French workmen to make fancy glass, and it is a fair guess that the French picked up the technique from wandering Venetians. As the Venetians began glass making where the Romans left off, and the Romans followed pretty closely the styles of ancient Syria, from there it is only a step to Egypt—and in the British Museum you will find some bottles made here 3,400 years ago using precisely this technique. Here you have one of the fascinating things about collecting; you buy some quite ordinary thing, perhaps just a frippery, and suddenly find it has links running right back through all the great empires of the past.

Another whole class of "Nailsea" consists of large pipes in coloured glass, made for hanging on walls or in the windows of tobacconists' shops, walking sticks, shepherds' crooks, coloured bell trumpets. But these have only the slenderest connections with Nailsea. Every glassmaking centre—Stourbridge, Sunderland, Bristol, York, and the

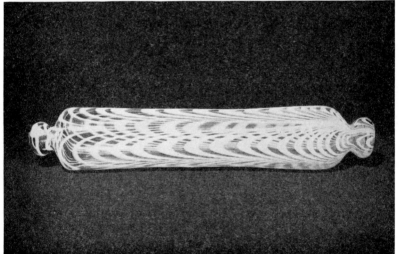

(*Top*) Little glass jugs of the sort that were sold at country markets and fairs in the late eighteenth and early nineteenth centuries (see page 35). All in the Victoria and Albert Museum, but similar ones can be bought today for about three to five pounds apiece.

(*Bottom*) "Nailsea" rolling pin with opaque white looped decoration, early nineteenth century (*Victoria and Albert Museum*).

rest—had their immense professional pride in making fantastic things of this sort, often for their annual processions. It is to be noted, too, that many of these things are still being made today, especially the coloured bells. The small toys also often attributed to Nailsea are dealt with under that head.

Much of the Nailsea stuff, whether it was made at Nailsea or not, was made for sale at country fairs and markets. Among the popular items there were the rolling pins, sometimes solid ones in the early bottle glass, sometimes hollow in clear or opaque glass bearing inscriptions. They seem to have been bought as keepsakes—often they are referred to as "sailors' charms"—filled with sweets or salt or tea and hung over the mantelpiece until the giver returned home again. This would be a very practical way of using them, for salt and tea cost money in those days, and needed to be kept dry. There was also another practical use, it seems, at any rate for the hollow ones with a stopper at one end. Our ancestors knew that not only is good pastry made with cool hands, but also with a cool rolling pin—which could be done by filling the roller with cold water. Certainly some modern manufacturers think so, for they make very efficient looking ones with extensions for your hands and screw stopper at one end.

But it seems that there was also another use for these pins, something which rather bears out the "charm" idea. Our ancestors, it is said, believed that not only was it unlucky to spill salt, but it was also asking for real trouble not to have any over the mantelpiece to stop the evil spirits coming down the chimney and into the house, so the rolling pin full of salt was always hung there. Of course, it would also have been very handy to have it where all the cooking was done.

Then there is the bottle or green glass doorstop, which seems to be more highly thought of by some people nowadays than Georgian glass, judging by the prices they are prepared to pay for such things. Imprisoned inside it was the

34

flower or plant, its leaves covered with tiny bubbles of air. Popular name for these was "dumps," and some even have a little flower pot with tiers of flowers coming up from it. These are being made again, so be careful what you buy or where you buy it.

Paperweights were also made in this bottle-glass but of course once we mention these articles we are off on a track which nowadays will either run us into a lot of money—or considerable disappointment. For just as newly made "dumps" can be bought in the Caledonian Market, so also mint-new paperweights from Italy can be found in quite respectable antique shops. The real weights, the collectors' fancy, from Stourbridge, Clichy, Baccarat, St. Louis, whether in millefiori, with its intricate geometrical arrangements of tiny tubes of coloured glass, or the, to me, much more delightful flowers forever embedded in their solid mounds of clear glass, have now moved to prices which, despite the enormous pains which were taken to make them are surely too high. So my advice is that if you go in for paperweights, do not look for bargains in the general shops, but make a careful study of the subject and buy in the top of the field.

Personally I would be more interested in those much more humble affairs—which can still be bought for shillings— where a coloured print of some long-superseded view is stuck on to the bottom of a mound of clear glass and shows through. They come in a variety of shapes, and preserve for us views and scenes we shall never see again.

But of all this "country fair" glass the things I love best, and would like to have a lot of, are the little mugs and jugs and vases which seem to be first cousins of all that charming "cottage" Staffordshire pottery of the eighteenth century. They are usually in bottle green, in purple or "Bristol" blue, in "milk and water" glass, as well as the proper opaque white glass. Some of them bear inscriptions, such as "Be canny with the Cream," but usually such gilding or enamelling has been worn off, and you are left with an irregular shape, touchingly simple and quite charming.

They seem to have been made towards the end of the eighteenth century and for the first thirty years of the nineteenth century, and were probably killed by the advance of factory methods such as pressing. At one time you could buy them quite cheaply, but now they will cost you three or four pounds for a plain one, more for those that have inscriptions. This may well be due to the fact that precisely similar things were made at the same era by glass-men in the United States—no doubt by emigrants from this country—and ours have consequently been sought by American collectors. But I believe they are still a good buy, for I do not suppose we shall ever again see such things made by craftsmen, not self-consciously as works of art, but for the everyday use and pleasure of ordinary folk.

3. *Victorian Fancies*

VICTORIAN fancy glass, in all its astonishing variety. Here is a field for the collector who likes pieces which can sometimes be gay and charming, sometimes elaborate and impressive, nearly always triumphs of glass-making skill which will probably never be made again. The group on the front cover shows a few of the types made.

But here as elsewhere the ordinary collector must specialise, otherwise he or she will be overwhelmed with all there is to buy. There are many ways of doing this— you can pick a particular process like spangled glass and collect specimens of it, or you can look for things of one kind, like vases or coloured glass plates. You could also make up combinations of them. But before going too far into selection let us see what there is to select.

CASED AND FLASHED GLASS

You will undoubtedly have seen imposing vases or decanters or lustres with pierced decoration which enables you to see through the top layers of glass to other colours underneath. This is what is known as cased or overlay glass, both of which words help a little to explain how the effect is achieved. They leapt into popularity about the middle of the nineteenth century, when the Bohemian glassmakers had a big success with them at the great Exhibition of 1851. Our own glasshouses very quickly climbed on to the wagon, and nowadays it is often difficult to know whether a piece was made in Bohemia or Stourbridge.

Cased glass is made by covering the basic glass vessel with one, two or even four layers of coloured glass, either clear or opaque and then cutting through the upper layers so as to reveal the ones beneath. There are many combinations of colours, and often the pieces are additionally decorated with gilding or enamelling. Good specimens with the enamelling still fresh are making high prices now wherever they come from. But personally I find the simpler English sorts preferable to the rather heavy Continental styles.

Another form of overlay much simpler to do and therefore cheaper, was called "flashed" glass. Here the basic glass vessel was allowed to cool, and instead of being inserted into a made "case" of glass, as with the more expensive process, it was quickly dipped into a pot of coloured glass. The film thus left on it could be cut through to show a pattern in the clear glass. One sees very attractive decanters and glasses which have been "flashed" with the popular ruby or amethyst, also some with several different colours, all incorporated in the etched or engraved design.

Transparent coloured glass comes in many forms. There is the dark blue called "Bristol"—though much of this was made elsewhere as well—like the enamelled blue jug and tumbler on the back cover. There are also several greens, there is a glorious deep purple which looks black until you hold it up to the light. Combinations of colours are found: there are ruby tea-sets or amber vases with scalloped decoration in clear class (on back cover). Sometimes you will come across a rather distinctive green with the not very attractive name of Vaseline Glass, though this does describe the colour pretty well. Chief items here are door-knobs, glass boxes, flower baskets, candlesticks and also some very fine ewers and basins. There is also a bluey-green glass with a smoky thread running through it, shown in the pair of candlesticks on the back cover.

(*Above left*) Flint glass vase, ruby flashed and cut. (*Above right*) Glass bowl, cased with opaque white overlay (*Courtesy "bits and pieces"*, 148 *Kensington Church St., London*). (*Below*) Bowl in "Nailsea" threaded and looped coloured glass, with applied decoration in the form of a blackthorn spray. Made about 1885 (*Courtesy Stourbridge Corporation*).

(*Right*) Opal glass lustre vase with cut flint-glass pendants. This type of vase, popular through the Victorian age right down to the present, is descended from the Georgian girandole, a table candelabra with hanging glass lustres or pendants.

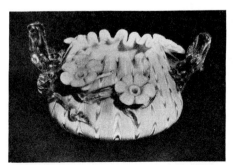

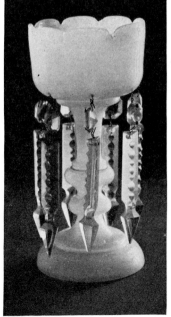

COLLECTABLE GLASS

MOTHER OF PEARL AND SATIN GLASS

Victorian glassmakers loved to play around with texture as well as colour, imitating other materials both in feel and appearance. Mother of pearl was much beloved by their customers, so they managed to get a finish which suggested it. One still sees a great deal of this Satin Glass, with its colours shading off into each other, say pale orange or pink into rose, or yellow into blue. Vases, candlesticks, nightlights, rose bowls and other items turn up frequently and one could make quite a show of them.

"Crizzling" and "crackling" was another favourite effect. This was done in the same sort of way as the crackle in Chinese porcelain. One sort of glass was "cased" with another, the inner one having a higher degree of expansion under heat than the outer one, with the result that the outer surface showed a multitude of tiny crackles, like a shattered car windscreen.

SPATTER, STRIPE AND SPANGLE

Here are three more recognisable types worth collecting. Spatter is a term you will hear when you are shown pieces which seem to be made of coloured glass with a mottled effect, with clear glass overlay and often having applied decoration of clear glass as well. Apart from candlesticks, there are sugar bowls, lamps, nightlights, even the little hats and shoes mentioned under "Toys." Then there is another type which comes in coloured stripes, opaque white in combination with pink, green or lemon. This also usually has an overlay of clear glass. Silvered glass gets its effect from having colouring matter between two skins of glass, the outer being cut away to reveal the silver.

Apart from the colour and texture effects, much was made

(*Above*) Goblet with opal thread pattern worked on Northwood's "pull-up" machine (see p. 42). Made about 1885.

(*Above right*) Candlestick with "latticinio" threading, made about 1888.

(*Below*) Bowl with a combination of "pull-up" threads and pillars of vertical coloured blobs. Made about 1886 (see p. 42) (*All by courtesy Stourbridge Corporation*).

of applied decoration with contrasting glass rosettes or leaves. The Venetian style ewer on the front cover has what are called "prunts" of little pink flowers; this is a family often seen in the shops. Similarly there was a popular line developed by Stevens and Williams in *verre-de-soie*, or satin glass, with decoration of acanthus leaves, the bent stem serving as the feet and the leaf being laid along the side of the piece in the most attractive way. There was also a little bowl (see page 39) in the "Nailsea" style of looped coloured glass with a blackthorn spray. In another style, taken from the Japanese, a rustic climbing spray is run up round a thin vase, with daisy rosettes stuck on all the way up.

Many of these pieces, as will be seen, are "crimped" at the top. This is often combined with patterns where glass colour threading is pulled up to make loops all round. There were also ingenious patterns made from small air bubbles.

OPAQUE AND PAINTED

Opaque or semi-opaque glass gives us a very large field indeed. I suppose that there are more blue and pink and green opaque glass vases on the dealers' shelves than any other kind of coloured glassware. Much of this is painted with flowers and pictures, often by lady amateurs working at home, for you could buy these vases plain and do your own decorating, as with china. Dark blue and black are often decorated with enamel painting, and it might be as well to say that the use of the word "enamel" glass for the opaque effect can be rather misleading. Opaque glass is usually achieved by the use of oxide of tin, in the same way as the glaze on delftware pottery, whereas true enamel is a sort of glass paint applied as a decoration.

Another rather confusing and much overworked word

(*Top right*) Victorian opaque white glass vase with hand-painted decoration (see page 42) of the sort often done by lady amateurs.

(*Below*) Edwardian "art nouveau" style rose coloured vase with streaked painting and silver mount.

(*Below right*) Mid-Victorian semi-opaque white glass vase painted with a pair of lovers, and gilded. Made at Lambeth (*Victoria and Albert Museum*).

in this connection is "Bristol" which you will hear applied to almost any kind of opaque glass. There was a glass, a beautiful opaque white, enamelled in colours which people often mistook for porcelain, which was undoubtedly made in Bristol in the eighteenth century, but it was made elsewhere as well. These cheaper sorts we have just been talking about may well have been made there, too, but much more came from Stourbridge and other glass centres.

Distinct from the completely opaque glass is opaline, with its fiery glow from transmitted light, and there are many attractive pieces of "milk and water" glass, like a window covered with frost.

With regard to arrangement, this is clearly cabinet or shelf collecting, but it seems to me that the first thing to decide is whether to go all out for one or other of these types, or whether to aim at a judicious mixture. I would be all in favour of the latter course, for to me the very variety and ingenuity of this coloured and decorated glass is its great charm. I would carefully look at it all before buying anything, and then carefully select pieces which will show each other off; buy a tall restrained opaline vase flanked by perhaps coloured lustre vases with clear glass drops, or a careful choice of clear coloured decanters and vases.

4. *Mary Gregory*

A FEW years ago you could have brought together a nice collection of Mary Gregory glass for quite a modest sum of money. Now you will have to pay for it—although if you chose carefully I should have thought that your purchases might still be a good investment. The general effect of a few shelves of it, in all its range of colours and subjects, could be an entrancing feature of any house.

First of all, what is Mary Gregory? And who was she?

From our illustration of a decanter on the front cover you will see that this name covers all those bottles, decanters, jugs, vases, glasses, small boxes and other pieces which have enamelled decoration showing children is unmistakably Victorian dress. Sometimes this enamelling is on clear glass, but the better work seems to be on the tinted glass—ruby, green, pink, blue, turquoise or amber. The children are charmingly of their period, and they bowl hoops, catch butterflies, fly kites, pick flowers from the garden, play games, sail boats and even climb up trees. Sometimes—though very rarely—you come across a pair of vases with a boy on one and a girl on the other, and there are even sets consisting of a decanter and six glasses—three boys and three girls.

But before you plunge in and buy, let us look a little more closely at the glass, and try to distinguish the good from the not so good. The best Mary Gregory that I have seen is the glass which was imported into this country from Bohemia (now Czechoslovakia) sometime in the middle of the nineteenth century.

It was also sent elsewhere, including the United States—which was how the "Mary Gregory" legend arose. The truth is that there *was* a Mary Gregory who did work like this at the Boston and Sandwich Glass works but she went in for it only after the arrival of the Bohemian glass in America. I have never to my knowledge seen a sample of her work—it would hardly have been exported to this country—so I do not know what stylistic differences there are between her work and the Bohemian. However, the better class of what we see in this country today is pretty clearly from the latter place, and apparently all from the same factory—that of Hahn, in Gablonz (Jablonec). It is on good quality glass, the decanters having fine stoppers, often gilded. Handles are sometimes elaborately blown, and there is an all-over feeling of the better class of Bohemian work of its time. The figures are always in white and there is a marked similarity in the features, as though the factory models were always followed very closely.

But there is another class of Mary Gregory about which is not nearly so fine. It is actually on poorer—and much more recent—glass, often clear white. The figures, especially the faces, are given flesh tints. No doubt these were intended to rival the Bohemian glass, but the white opaque painting is much to be preferred, for this is not a suitable subject for realistic treatment—half the charm is gone.

From what has been said about the colours of the glass—some of the tints are very fine indeed—this is obviously a collection which needs good light, and as so often with glass the best way to do this is to let the light come through the pieces, either with artificial lighting or by placing your shelves out in the room.

If you have one of those peeping windows in the hall which don't open, this could be ideal for your family of Mary Gregory children.

5. *Slagware*

FOR some years now prices have been steadily rising for a kind of ware which many of its buyers often do not realise is glass at all.

Perhaps most people will recognise it when I say that there are vases and boxes in a very characteristic sort of pale blue, with designs which appear to have been pressed from moulds. This blue is quite unmistakable, and although at one time one had to hunt for these pieces, nowadays they are very carefully brought out for your inspection and arranged in sets.

Blue is not the only colour, of course: there is also a family in cream, in plain white and in something which looks like black until you hold it to the light, when it shows amethyst. There is also another type which has a sort of marbled effect of purple or green and white. People often mistake all this ware for some sort of china, and it doesn't help them when they find dealers referring to it as slagware. Another name sometimes given to it is "end-of-the-day" ware, while still other authorities, including one of its makers, refer to it as "vitro-porcelain."

I prefer the name "end-of-the-day" not only because it sounds nicer, but also because it gives a clue as to how the ware is said to have been made. Apparently the glass-makers bought silicates from steel-works in the form of the slag drawn off molten steel, and mixed this with clear glass. The name comes from the fact that the slag was drawn off at the end of the day; and this sounds a much more likely story than the other explanation of the name, that the pieces

47

used up all the odd bits of glass left over at the end of the day.

One of the comforting things about this ware is that you can often trace it to a maker by the Registry Mark found on some pieces (see page 50). This is a diamond-shaped mark which is often found on pottery, giving the year and month and parcel number of the design. From the records (now in the custody of the Victoria and Albert Museum, London) you can discover the name of the firm registering the design. Of the pieces in our picture for example, the large white fish jug is registered by W. H. Heppell and Co., Newcastle, in 1882; while the larger of the pinched baskets, on the right, which is cream coloured, was made by the principal firm in the trade, Sowerby's Ellison Glass Works, also of Newcastle-upon-Tyne, who also registered the name "vitro-porcelain." This piece also bears the firm's own mark, which was a peacock's head, and is often found without the Registry Mark.

Apart from the vases and spill holders, there is a very attractive series of flat-sided flasks impressed with pictures, mostly based on nursery stories. I saw one fairly recently with an illustration of "Jack and Jill" on offer for £4 10s. and as it was gone a few days later, this was presumably the market price.

Heaviest demand is for the marbled types and in fact here is another name; many go in exclusively for this, calling it Marble Ware glass. Colours have a much wider range than is commonly imagined, for apart from the more usual purple and green there are also blue, orange and a sort of butterscotch colour. Favourite items are small jugs, covered dishes, pitchers, creamers, cake stands, tumblers, bowls, trays, match holders, compotes, butter dishes. The large celeries and covered sugars are getting almost impossible to find now.

But if you are the sort of collector who likes to start at the modest end of the field and work your way up, why not look at some of the more ambitious versions of this sort of

Some pieces of slagware, or "vitro-porcelain," the name registered by Sowerby's Ellison Glass Works, Newcastle-upon-Tyne. Described on the facing page, this ware was also made by many small firms on Tyneside.

marbled ware. There was a Bohemian glass called "Lythyalin" which was produced in the 1820's; it showed marble patterns in vivid colours, while a similar product called "Hyalith" appeared in sealing-wax red and a dense opaque black. Specimens of these wares turn up sometimes at the London auctions.

Chinese glass not only tries marbled effects but also often imitates materials like red laquer, onyx, chalcedony and jade. This was also done at Venice, and turns up here under the German name *Schmelzglas*: there are some beautiful ewers and bottles. I saw one the other day which was enriched with *avanturine*, that charming decoration related to spangled glass, so called because the bright flecks of gold in the glass went wherever they "adventured" to do.

COLLECTABLE GLASS

As a rough guide to the date of any piece you may have, look first at the top of the diamond. The Roman numeral (IV) indicates the class, in this case "Glass and Ceramics." If there is a letter immediately underneath this, i.e., in the semi-circle just inside the diamond, the piece was made between 1842 and 1867, according to the following table:

Years

1842	X	1849	S	1856	L	1863	G
1843	H	1850	V	1857	K	1864	N
1844	C	1851	P	1858	B	1965	W
1845	A	1852	D	1859	M	1866	Q
1846	I	1853	Y	1860	Z	1867	T
1847	F	1854	J	1861	R		
1848	U	1855	E	1862	O		

If, however, there is a figure in this place, and the letter appears on the left-hand corner of the diamond, then it was made between 1868 and 1883, according to the following table:

Years

1868	X	1872	I	1876	V	1880	J
1869	H	1873	F	1877	P	1881	E
1870	C	1874	U	1878	D	1882	L
1871	A	1875	S	1879	Y	1883	K

6. Glass Toys

IF you go to Stourbridge to watch the glassmakers, as I suggested you should do when talking about cut glass, see if you can find one of the small workshops where they still make glass toys "at the lamp."

Here you will find people working over a jet of gas with rods or tubes of coloured and clear glass, of specially soft quality, which they twist or blow into all kinds of shapes and figures. This is the source of those fantastic figures and animals, even whole fields of huntsmen, horses and dogs, which one finds in the shops.

Glass is a wonderfully suitable material for making conceits and fancies in this way, and it is no wonder that this branch of the industry has been going on for centuries, nor that glassblowers in the main houses have always liked to show off their skill in blowing and manipulating small pieces. People working in the glass trade used to call these things "friggers," but of course nowadays it is difficult to know whether a piece was produced "off hand" in this way or made in the ordinary way of business over a lamp.

Anyway there are the engaging pieces to collect, and many families they fall into. There are small hats in clear glass or in colours—bowlers, curly-brimmed top hats, jockeys' caps, firemen's helmets, clowns' hats, many of them meant as toothpicks or match holders. There are glass eggs, said to be used as handcoolers, glass boots, shoes and slippers, the last, I believe given to brides when they set off on their fateful journey. Many of these things were not originally designed as ornaments, at least not primarily

—you could have slippers, boots and shoes in the form of bottles holding perfume, ink or beer.

But for anyone who can be enchanted with the really tiny, there are all those little wares made for dolls houses, much smaller than china ones. There are tea-sets, bottles, decanters, jugs, dishes and plates which seem to have been made for Queen Mab herself, for they certainly come

> "In shape no bigger than an agate-stone
> On the forefinger of an alderman."

I have seen them in "Nailsea" stripes, in "Bristol" blue and opaque glass, in opaline, in fact in practically every sort used in making their larger fellows. It is amazing sometimes, how closely they follow the styles of their various periods, as though the children of those days, who looked

Bottle in the form of a toy pistol, one of the many different forms used for containers of sweets, scents, liquors, etc., in days gone by.

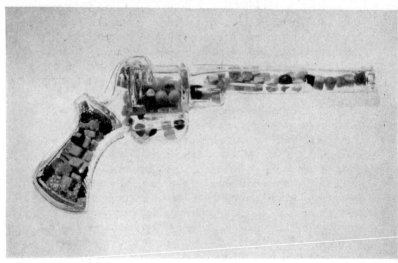

A small glass ship (8 in. by 6 in.) made of fine threads of spun flint and blue
glass. Made in Bristol, first half of nineteenth century (*Victoria and Albert
Museum*). Birds, coaches, fountains and other objects can be made in this way
by heating glass rods at a flame and spinning the glass out to an extraordinary
fineness.

like miniature replicas of grown-ups in their dress, wanted
their dolls ware also to be exact replicas of what mamma
and papa used in their dining room. Amazing too,
considering the bad tempers sometimes shown in nurseries,
that so many have survived. But I suspect too that many
were bought by grown-ups for their charm and interest.

If you do go in for these little things, however, you will

COLLECTABLE GLASS

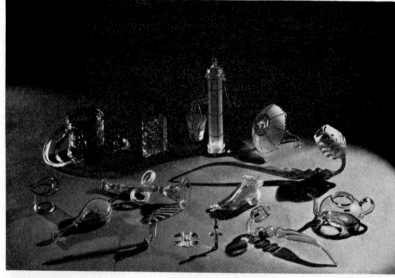

A group of glassmakers' "friggers" from the Stourbridge Corporation glass collection.

have to be very eagle-eyed, for they often get "lost" with other things. In one of the big London salerooms the other day I saw a cardboard box containing perhaps twenty various miniature pieces of glass—in a sale of *porcelain*.

The glass animals, birds and so on, which are such a feature of the fancy goods and glass shops today are a long history—and no doubt will one day be as eagerly collected as its predecessors. As far back as the seventeenth century, glassmakers at Nevers in France were modelling little figures of animals and people and making them up into groups such as a Crucifixion. One country or another has continued this tradition right down to the present. Even last Christmas I pulled a cracker with a nephew and found in it an enchanting little gazelle made of some kind

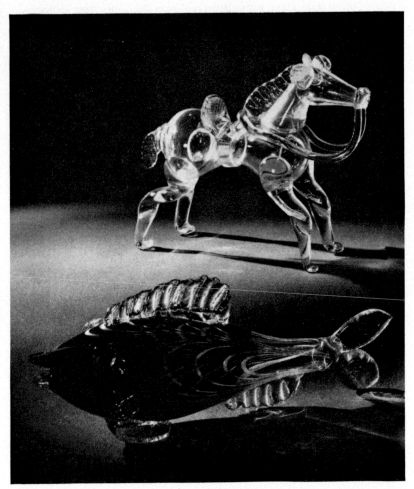

Hollow hand-blown horse in clear glass and fish in pale ruby cased inside with white opal festooned thread. Designed and made in 1950 by Habets Marten for Stevens and Williams, Brierley Hill.

of opaque glass, quite different from the types seen in the shops.

There were replicas of things like umbrellas, flower pieces, tiny swords and musical instruments, which people bought in the nineteenth century as small gifts for children.

Much more ambitious, but still, I suppose, to be classified as toys, are the wonderfully intricate models of ships, their rigging made of spun glass. These as well as fountains with birds and, indeed, if one is to believe their advertisements, any kind of toy, were made by the itinerant glassmakers travelling the countryside with their lamps and rods of glass.

Sometimes it is possible to pick up quite a nice little lot of toys at sales. At Sothebys in 1960 this lot went for only ten pounds: a white opaque guild pipe with a ruby rim (no doubt one of those used in processions), a blue-glass snake weight with gilt markings, a clear glass fluted trumpet, a dark blue and clear glass snake-headed lazy-tong ornament, a green glass pig flask, a clear glass pipe, a bellows flask, two flasks with latticinio decoration, three gild walking sticks, and a crystallo-ceramic profile head of Wellington in papier mâché frame.

7. *Some Foreigners*

THE title of this chapter is meant in no disparaging sense. English glassmakers have always been interested in what went on abroad, even if for a very long time they put most of their energies stubbornly into making a special glass of lead, heavily cut, which beat some of the Continental people in their own markets. But in the same way, the imposing flashed and cased Bohemian glass sent here in 1851, was most respectfully copied by Stourbridge, as were some of the Venetian styles.

Plenty of this German glass turns up at the auctions, so it may be worth while drawing attention to a few types. We have already mentioned the marbled "Hyalith" and "Lythyalin" under *Slagware*. There is also a great deal of enamelled opaque glass of the same kind as Bristol though with very different decoration, under the name *milchglass*. The green Rhenish glass is famous, and is often found as roemers (first cousins to our rummers), and used for the white wines of the Rhineland. The long stems usually have what the Germans called *nuppen*, but the English glassmakers call "prunts," or little raspberries of glass stuck all the way up the stems, presumably to give the drinker a better grip on the glass. Another old German glass occasionally seen is the *Kuttrolf*, or *angster*, which has several intertwined tubular necks which meet in the wide mouth. Apparently it is used in the same sort of way as the Spanish *biberon*, to pour out a little at a time. Then there are all the tall cups and goblets. The *passglass* was one with levels shown on the decoration to indicate how much you were expected to drink before passing it on, while a tall cylindrical beaker was called a *stangenglass* (pole-glass) often covered over with points, when it became an *Igel* (hedgehog) glass. This developed into the family of *humpen* or tall beer glasses, among them the Willkomm—(welcome) humpen and the Reichsadler (imperial eagle) humpen.

An interesting form of decoration was that known as *schwartzlot*, a method of painting in black with touches of red and there are some very fine landscapes, figures and hunting scenes. Still another term heard in the salerooms is *Zwischengoldglass*, a literal rendering of how a gold decoration is entrapped between two skins of glass, both at the sides and the bottom. It is to be remembered, however, that a good deal of German glass was made *à la façon de Venice*, that is to say, after the fashion of Venice—Germans, Austrians, Bohemians and Dutchman all being strongly influenced not only by the glass coming out of Venice but by the renegade Venetian glassmakers coming out of there, too.

While on Venice one might draw attention to the Stourbridge ewer illustration on the front cover. This bears a strong resemblance to a Venetian ewer in the Victoria and Albert Museum, and well illustrates the fact that where Germany and Bohemia tended to be solid, heavy and immensely expert in decoration, Venetian glass, both in substance and treatment, was light, graceful and airy. Specialities of the Venetian style are the white or coloured threads of *latticinio*, mentioned under "Nailsea"; and the *millefiori* used famously in paperweights in France and Stourbridge. More intricate patterns are called *vetro de trina*, or lace glass. Another favourite Venetian production was ice-glass, whereby the surface of the glass was frosted or crazed by sudden immersion in water and reheating. Outstanding productions of Venice are *tazza*, or stands on stems rather like our cakestands, but with the most elaborate and delicate arrangement of foliage, animals, birds and other extravagances.

(*Right*) Nineteenth century Venetian style ewer, with "wrythen" body and serpentine-entwined handle, embellished with "prunts" of flowers.

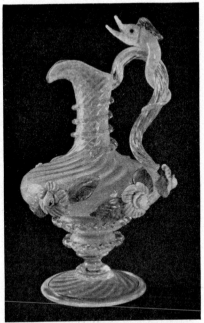

(*Below right*) Late nineteenth century French semi-opaque glass, with applied decoration in "art nouveau" style, perhaps about 1900.

(*Below*) Bohemian nineteenth century glass. The slender vase is flashed ruby and cut, while the tall bottle-shaped one is "cased," with gilding on the clear glass panels.

(*All by courtesy "bits and pieces"*).

French glass often seen in England includes what was known here as "art glass." Once upon a time we frowned upon the work of Emile Gallé, with its cloudy effects of light and colour, its wonderful naturalism in flowers and plant life, making most ingenious use of almost every process mentioned in this book and several others as well. His *clair de lune*, or moonlight glass, is famous, as is his *verre double*, in which the effects were obtained by repeated flashings. Réné Lalique's glass has been popular in this country ever since it started to come here at the beginning of the century. His most effective work depends upon a beautiful glass, a fine mat surface and bold modelling. French work in paperweights has been mentioned and it might be remembered that the "crystallo-cramie," or sulphides, made by Apsley Pellat showing cameo portraits enclosed in crystal glass, originated in France.

Sometimes extravagant examples of Spanish glass turn up, and sometimes Persian and Syrian items, bearing the patina of the years. But one of these days, when I have the money, I am going to buy myself a small collection of those delightful glass phials and bottles, in shapes that must have been inspired by the pixies, which the English or Romano-British glassmakers turned out in hundreds, then carefully allowed to lie in the earth for hundreds of years and acquired a unique greeny silvery sheen which is almost as wonderful as their shapes.

8. Bottled History

LOOKING at the row of old bottles on page sixty-three some people might well wonder what possible interest or attraction they might have. Surely the only person likely to collect them would be a dustman!

Yet anyone with a taste for history and interest in old things can find a fascinating quest in old serving bottles—or "sealed" bottles as they are sometimes called. For in many cases it is possible not only to date them but to trace their actual owner anything up to three hundred years ago.

These bottles go back to the time when an establishment of any consequence—a big house or a college—would buy its wine by the barrel, and have it brought to the tables in bottles. At first these bottles, short, round and dumpy, were made of stoneware or delftware and they often bore the initials or arms of the original owner, a date, and sometimes the name of the wine, say Rhenish or Sack.

But in the first part of the seventeenth century a monopoly was set up for the manufacture of glass in England, and as a result of the rapid development of the industry, these earthenware bottles began to be displaced by others in the dark greeny brown of what we now call "bottle" glass. In fact this is the natural glass, before it is "washed" into the clear material used for better quality wares.

For many people the attraction of the old bottles lies in their shapes, which are sometimes wonderfully irregular and haphazard, sometimes finely and nobly proportioned. But what draws other collectors to them is the fact that in many cases their original owners carried on—from the earlier earthenware bottles—the practice of having their initials or crest or even names on them, quite often with a date, in the form of a glass "seal" or lozenge. Sometimes the name of the house is given, for example "Picton Castle" or "Boxted Hall," while a great many towns and villages appear, also the initials of university colleges.

There must still be many of these bottles lurking about in unsuspected places, for I have heard of several being discovered in old cellars quite recently. I myself bought two a year or so ago. One of them has the seal of a baronet, a Sir William Strickland, of Boynton, Yorkshire. As well as his name it bears the date 1809: on looking the gentlemen up I find that this was a year or two after he succeeded to the baronetcy. His bottle cost me 35s.

The smaller one marked "Trelaske" created a great deal of interest when I asked in an article if anyone knew a place of this name. Many correspondents wrote in to point out that it was an old house in Cornwall, and in fact the actual owner, who had recently moved in and was renovating the place, wrote to ask if I would sell him the bottle—which I gladly did. Another interesting development was that a lady living on a farm a few miles away from Trelaske wrote to say that she had found there an old bottle with the seal "Samuel Archer," this being the name of the family which once lived at Trelaske. Another bottle in the picture, which I borrowed from a friend to make up the "bottle-scape" bears the initials "I.W." I like to think that this was one of those that Izaak Walton carried down to the river with him.

As so many of these bottles are dated, it is possible to trace the evolution of the shapes down the centuries. As already mentioned, the early ones were "dumpies," little round ones with a long neck. This gradually became modified when people began to lay down their wines for keeping, and needed the bottles to be cylindrical shaped, so that they would lie on their sides.

At least one famous person had his seal. In her book

A group of "sealed" and other collectable bottles. The two outside ones with handles are wine-flagons, probably of foreign origin. The squat one on its side has no seal, but its shape puts it earlier in date, probably, than the two sealed ones standing beside it. Of these, the one behind bears the initials "I.W.," the other "Sir William Strickland, Bart, 1809." To its left is a square-shouldered "case" bottle, for packing in boxes or chests, found in Bristol and probably dating from about 1800. The other sealed bottle bears the name "Trelaske," a house in Cornwall—to which it has recently been restored.

"Sealed Bottles" the late Sheelah Ruggles-Brice not only gave a long list of seals, tracing some of their owners, but quotes the fact that Mr. Samuel Pepys notes in his diary in 1663: "Went to Mr. Rawlinson's and saw some of my new bottles, made with my crest upon them, filled with wine, about five or six dozen." It is interesting to see that here the wine merchant is selling the wine not in bulk, but in bottles specially made for the client, and presumably re-filled as necessary. Similarly, merchants and inn keepers would also have their own marked bottles, and use them for serving customers either "on or off the premises."

Eventually, of course, when vintners began supplying wine in bottles for keeping, and decanters were used at the table, the sealed serving bottles of the gentry went out of use. But they must have lingered on a long time in the taverns, for some have dates as late as the 1850's.

Well, as I say, not everybody will want to fill their lounges with bottles of this kind, and it seems to me that this is one of those collecting subjects for the "den," or better still, a cellar. The bottles will hardly come to any harm there. But why not do as quite a few people do nowadays, buy your wine in bulk. You can then lay it down in these bottles. I am sure they would be much happier doing their job than standing empty for another century or so.

Some Useful Books

GLASS. W. B. Honey. Victoria and Albert Museum, 1949.

JOHN NORTHWOOD. John Northwood II. Mark and Moody Ltd., Stourbridge, 1956.

ENGLISH GLASS. W. A. Thorpe. A. and C. Black, 1949.

GLASS THROUGH THE AGES. E. Barrington Haynes. Penguin Books, 1959.

ENGLISH GLASS FOR THE COLLECTOR: 1660–1860. C. Bernard Hughes. Lutterworth Press, 1958.

VICTORIAN GLASS. Ruth Webb Lee. Framingham Centre, Mass. (U.S.A.).

ENGLISH TABLEGLASS. E. M. Elville. Country Life Ltd., 1951.

PAPERWEIGHTS AND OTHER GLASS CURIOSITIES. E. M. Elville. Country Life Ltd., 1952.